MORE THAN
AMAZING
GRACE

YOUR STRUGGLE IS OVER

GREGORY DICKOW

More than Amazing Grace

Your Struggle Is Over

Printed in the United States of America

For information, please write

Gregory Dickow Ministries
PO Box 7000
Chicago, IL 60680

or visit us online at www.gregorydickow.org.

Table of Contents

MORE THAN AMAZING GRACE

When I met Jesus, I didn't promise Him that I would change—that's religion. He promised He would change me—that's grace! I'll tell you more about that in a few minutes . . .

But you see, what I want to share with you today is that the Christian life is not about the promises we make to God, but rather it is about the promises He makes to us!

This grace is what brought me to Jesus, has kept me walking with Him, and has changed my life from the inside out.

No matter what is going on in your life right now, the most important thing you can do is to STOP trying so hard to change. Stop beating yourself up for your flaws, shortcomings, and failures. Condemnation doesn't lead us to the Lord, it pushes us away. Condemnation and frustration doesn't change us. Love changes us. Grace changes us.

I love what Romans 2:4 says: It is the goodness—the lovingkindness of God—that leads us to Him, and leads us to repentance, or to change.

When I was about 17 years old, I attended a Bible study for the first time. Even though I got saved that night, I couldn't stop doing the things I was doing. I couldn't stop drinking or doing drugs. I couldn't stop feeling depressed or getting angry.

So frankly, I gave up trying to change. I hope you don't get the wrong idea. I wanted to live the Christian life, but it seemed too hard.

What made me stop trying so hard to change? It wasn't working! I kept going back to the way I was no matter how hard I tried. I kept stumbling over the same things, and the things in my life remained the same. But when I got a hold of what I'm sharing with you, everything changed.

Romans 12:2 says, "Do not be conformed to this world but be transformed by the renewing of your mind." To *be transformed*, describes what is done TO YOU. It literally means to be changed from the inside out. It is where we get the word, *metamorphosis*, from. When a caterpillar is transformed on the inside into a butterfly, it's not something that the caterpillar does to himself. It is something that is DONE TO the caterpillar. No caterpillar becomes a butterfly just because he wishes he were a butterfly, or dreams about it everyday. It is something that happens to him.

Today just start doing what the caterpillar does. He spins a cocoon and rests inside. The Creator takes it from there. Let what you read in this book become a cocoon for you. Let this grace thinking wrap around your head and heart.

God's Word will change your thinking, and transformation will happen TO you. That's grace.

I love what Zechariah said, in chapter 4:7. We are to shout GRACE GRACE to the mountain. Not WORK WORK or LAW LAW, but GRACE GRACE!

The Christian life is a life of recognition, a life of acknowledging the victory that is already ours, through what Jesus already did.

Philemon, verse 6, says that our faith becomes effective by acknowledging (not obtaining) every good thing ALREADY in us, by Christ Jesus. The grace, love, and blessing of God is already yours in Christ. As we acknowledge them and thank God that they are already ours, our faith soars. We reign in life. And when you believe that, everything is going to be all right!

Chapter One

It Is Finished

*"Therefore when Jesus had received the sour wine, He said,
'It is finished!' And He bowed His head and gave up
His spirit" (John 19:30).*

**Grace is all about the finished work of Jesus on the
cross. And when I think about the finished work of
Jesus on the cross, I am home!** When I hear the echo
of those words Jesus spoke hanging from the cross—IT
IS FINISHED, **I realize I have arrived**—not to perfec-
tion, obviously, but to a place of spiritual rest and peace.
No more striving. No more sweating. No more trying to
get right with God through my efforts. No more making
promises to be holy, to be better, to clean up my act. No
more trying to pick up the pieces of a broken life. He *makes*
me holy. He *makes* me better. He cleans me up. He picks
up the broken pieces and makes me whole again. IT IS
FINISHED. This is the grace of God.

"Grace" is God's unmerited love and favor. A great
acronym for G.R.A.C.E. is:

God's

Riches

At

Christ's

Expense.

The same grace that saves us is also the grace that empowers us, heals us, and transforms us. Everything we need in life flows from the gift of God's grace. And that grace is given to us through the finished work of Jesus on the cross. There is NOTHING we can do to earn it, work for it, or deserve it. It is a gift, settled forever because of the cross.

The world of religion (man's efforts to be made right with God), even among Christians, is often confused and misguided where grace is concerned. We are often "New Testament" in our hearts, but still "Old Testament" in our heads. In other words, we know we are born again when we accept Jesus, but we THINK we have to take it from there, and fix our lives, clean our lives, and bring God's promises to pass through our efforts or holiness. We have it backward.

It's almost as if many Christians are suffering from spiritual dyslexia, where we are reading God's truths backward! It's as if we feel we have to make promises to Him, in order for Him to keep His promises to us.

But in Revelation 1:5–6, we see the grace of God in full display when John describes the beautiful work of Jesus in our lives. "To Him who loved us and washed us from our sins in His own blood, and has made us kings and priests to His God and Father . . ." (NKJV).

Let's not get this backward.

Notice the order of how God's grace works in our lives:

1. He loved us. This is first.

2. He washed us.

3. He made us kings and priests.

You see, God doesn't love what is washed. He washes what He loves! He loves us first, and that's WHY He washes us in His own blood. And that's WHY He raises us up, making us kings and priests. He loves us first. He does good to us first.

Let me give you an example of what I'm talking about: where we get it backward, and we don't understand God's "more than amazing grace."

Repentance doesn't lead to God's blessing and goodness (that's backward!) God's goodness and blessing leads us to repentance.

When Jesus meets up with Peter in His boat, He tells him to launch out into the deep.

Luke 5:6–7: "They let down their net and they caught a great number of fish, and their net began to break! So they signaled to their partners in the other boat for them to come and help them. And they came and filled both of the boats, so that they began to sink."

You see, Peter encounters this net-breaking, boat-sinking, supernatural goodness of God. And THEN what happened?

Vs. 8, "When Simon Peter saw *it* . . ." (When he saw God's grace and blessing towards this cussing sailor!) "He fell down at Jesus feet and said, 'Depart from me Lord, I'm a sinful man'."

In other words, God showed up in Peter's boat and BLESSED him beyond measure with His goodness and grace; and it LED to Peter's repentance. Peter's repentance was a REFLEX to God's goodness.

Religion says, "C'mon, Peter. Fall at Jesus's feet, and THEN He'll fill your boat." But Jesus says: "Let me fill up your boat with no strings attached." And Peter's spiritual reflex is to fall to his knees.

This is what the Bible means when it says: "For it is the goodness (grace, lovingkindness) of God that leads us to repentance" (Romans 2:4).

Someone wrote me recently, saying, "Dear Pastor Dickow, As you have been ministering on the grace and goodness of God, and that is being solidified in my mind as His nature and character, I have found it leading me to go to Him to pray and ask even more."

You see, first we *understand* Jeremiah 29:11—and discover God is good and not evil, that He thinks good towards us, and has good plans for us and our future.

Then, as a result—as a reflex—we *experience* Jeremiah 29:12. "Then you will call upon Me and go and pray to Me, and I will listen to you."

You see, it's God's grace and His goodness that draws us into a deeper relationship with Him: a greater desire to pray, listen, and follow Him.

You WANT to go to and spend time with someone who thinks good of you, plans the best for you, and has good hopes for your future. Whereas in life, we avoid relationships and fellowship with people who have a negative mindset toward us, hold small thoughts toward our future, or doubt and are skeptical toward the greatness that God has planned!

But we RUN into the arms of the One who is good, and does good, and holds nothing back from us in His unrestrained, uncontained, unstoppable love and grace!

This is why the devil works overtime to push a wrong concept of God. He wants to keep us from running into the arms of the God of all grace. When you discover who He really is, as evidenced through His unconditional love and sacrifice, you can't help but love Him. We love Him, BECAUSE He first loved us (1 John 4:19).

Religion tells us we have to strive and struggle and fight to be pleasing to God, to receive His blessings, and to experience our destiny. While we exert our efforts to obtain God's approval, blessing, and power, we BURN OUT and get frustrated in this false form of Christianity.

It's time to stop burning out and start burning brighter!

Chapter Two

Grace to You!

"Grace to you and peace from Him who is and who was and who is to come" (Revelation 1:4).

It goes without saying that the book of Revelation is one of the most important books of the Bible. All Scripture is inspired and God-breathed, but the message to the churches of what may be the last days, is especially vital to understand.

John was the closest disciple to Jesus. We know he was the one who leaned upon the chest of Jesus. We know he had a revelation of God's love. We know he was the only disciple who didn't run away when Jesus was being crucified. He stood at the foot of the cross the whole time. This was a special man with a special message.

Exiled to the island of Patmos, because Rome failed in their attempts to kill him, there in isolation, John receives from Jesus the Revelation to the churches, the Revelation of the last days—the Omega book of the Bible!

And so the message of Revelation could not be more relevant and important to understand. There are many things left to interpretation in this glorious book. But make no mistake, the first words of this book set the tone for what God is saying to us now, in the remaining time we are on this earth, and until Jesus comes.

Notice the first words from John in this book:

"*Grace to you* and peace from Him who is and who was and who is to come" (Revelation 1:4).

The first 3 words are essential. This is the New Testament message. This is the message for these days and any days:

Grace to you!

The first thing Jesus is saying to John is: Grace to you!

The first thing John is saying to us is: Grace to you!

The first thing God wants us to hear is: Grace to you!

There's nothing more important to understand than that God's grace is *for* you and *to* you!

Grace is: God's unconditional love and unmerited favor toward us.

He doesn't say: Law to you. Religion to you. Rules to you. Do's and Don'ts to you. He says: GRACE TO YOU!

This is what God is sending to us daily: GRACE to you. This is what the churches of today need to be filled with.

This is what needs to hit everyone the moment they walk through the doors of our churches: Grace to you.

This is what needs to flow to us and through us: Grace to you.

This is why many people avoid church. They feel judgment to them, rather than grace to them. We are sending messages of self-righteousness to them; rather than grace to them. We are sending messages of "clean up your act" to them, rather than grace to them.

People aren't running to churches because church has become a place for where only the "holy" should go. You'll be judged if you look like you don't have it together.

Jesus didn't greet anyone with fear or anger. He greeted them with grace. Jesus greets us with grace. And He instructs John to greet us with grace. Grace to you! Grace is the beginning of the life God has for you. Its the beginning of all of His plans that He has for you. Notice how well the Apostle Paul understands this grace: He opens the book of Romans, 1 Corinthians, 2 Corinthians, Galatians, Ephesians, Philippians, Colossians, 1 and 2 Thessalonians, 1 and 2 Timothy, Titus and Philemon with this same declaration: **GRACE TO YOU!** (Romans 1:7, 1 Cor 1:3, 2 Cor 1:2, Gal 1:3, Eph 1:2, Phil 1:2, Col 1:2, 1 Thess 1:1 and 2 Thess 1:2, 1 Tim 1:2, 2 Tim 1:2, Titus 1:4, Philemon 1:3). It's staggering to think that every epistle written by Paul starts with GRACE TO YOU. Do you think God is trying to get a message across to us? Every letter, every instruction, the revealing of God's written will to us—starts with grace. These are not just meant to be nice greetings. These declarations of grace in each of these New Testament letters is sending a message to us. It's setting the course of how God intends for us to think and live: with an abundance of GRACE TO US.

Grace to you means God's grace comes TO us. We can't obtain it. We can't go get it. We can't earn it. We can't go find it. We can't chase it down. Its coming to you. It's chasing you. It's following you, ALL THE DAYS OF YOUR LIFE!

We can't save ourselves, heal ourselves, or deliver ourselves. Grace does that. Grace comes to you and saves you by the blood of Jesus. Grace comes to you and heals you by His stripes.

Remember G.R.A.C.E. = God's Riches At Christ's Expense.

Grace is the great exchange!

He was made sin so that we could be made the righteousness of God (2 Corinthians 5:21).

He was cursed on the cross, so that we could be blessed in this life and forever (Galatians 3:13–14).

He took our sickness on His back, so that by His stripes we could be healed (1 Peter 2:24).

He became poor that we through His poverty could be made rich (2 Corinthians 8:9).

Notice this verse defining the spirit of grace:

For you know the grace of our Lord Jesus Christ, that though He was rich, yet for your sake He became poor, so that you through His poverty might become rich (2 Corinthians 8:9).

This is how we know the grace of our Lord Jesus—there is a clear and undeserved exchange. He became what we were so that we could become what He was, before He became what we were!

GRACE PRODUCES POWER AND PEACE

The more grace you allow to come to you, the more power will come to you.

"For the grace of God has appeared to all men, bringing salvation, **training us** to renounce ungodliness and worldly passions, and to live self-controlled, upright, and godly lives in the present age" (Titus 2:11–12).

As you discover the *grace to you*, His grace trains us, which means it enables and empowers us to live godly lives.

One more thought about this verse in Revelation 1:4 before we move on. It says, "Grace to you; and peace." You see? Once you discover grace, then peace comes. Peace is always the reflex of grace. Because grace comes to you, peace always follows.

The primary reason we don't enjoy the peace that God intended for us is because we don't understand grace. Grace leads to peace and so much more!

Chapter Three

The Battle Is Over

"Comfort my people. Declare that her
warfare is over!" (Isaiah 40:1–2)

Jesus did it all! That's grace.

The war with the devil, death, sin and destruction is OVER. We don't need to fight an enemy that is already defeated.

Romans 5:17 says, "Through the abundance of grace and the gift of righteousness, we REIGN in life."

It doesn't say, "We are *trying* to reign through grace and righteousness." It says: WE REIGN.

Jesus defeated the devil. Our part is to resist the devil with the truth of God's Word and our authority. Jesus redeemed us from the curse. Our part is to "let the redeemed SAY SO!" (Psalm 107:2)

We have to stop trying to obtain a victory that we already have. That doesn't mean we don't have a battle to fight. But the battle that we fight is to resist wrong thinking and wrong believing. Jesus defeated the devil! And He gave us authority over him and over all the power of the enemy!

"Behold I give you authority . . . over all the power of the enemy and nothing shall by any means harm you!" (Luke 10:19)

Why are so many believers failing and living defeated lives? Because they lack the knowledge of the victory that they already have.

You see, in the Old Testament, the people of God praised their way TO the victory. But in this MORE THAN AMAZING New Testament, we praise God FROM the victory.

Jehosaphat sent the praisers out against the enemy, and as they praised God, the enemy routed each other (2 Chronicles 20:22–23). But we don't send out our praise to try to get the victory—that's Old Testament thinking. We praise God because we already have the victory in Christ! That's New Testament thinking. Do you see the difference?

We don't worship God to usher our way into His presence. We worship Him, BECAUSE He brought us into His presence through the blood of Jesus! (Hebrews 10:19)

MORE THAN CONQUERORS

"Nay, in all these things we are more than conquerors through Him that loved us!" (Romans 8:37)

You see, we are not trying to conquer. We are MORE than conquerors. A conqueror conquers. But someone who is MORE than a conqueror simply enters into the victory that has already been won. Jesus was the conqueror. He conquered sin, the devil, the curse, and death! And He gave us the victory, making us MORE than conquerors. We get all the rewards and benefits of victory, without having to fight for it.

Our battle is to believe this incredible, amazing, overwhelmingly good Gospel! This is winning in spiritual warfare: to agree with God, to accept what He has ALREADY done for us. It's to believe it and receive it, NOT try to achieve it. He did the achieving. We simply do the believing and receiving! The battle is in our thinking. Whatever thoughts don't agree with God's finished work of grace, are the thoughts we must take captive and cast down (2 Corinthians 10:3–5).

Now, lets look more closely at how much better we have it in this New Testament grace.

Chapter Four

A Better Covenant

In order to understand the Gospel of grace—the too-good-to-be-true good news—we need to see the brilliance of God and the picture He paints of our victory in the Old Testament. It is a picture, the shadow of the REAL THING (Hebrews 8:5, Hebrews 10:1). They had the shadow of the Man and it was awesome. We have the Man! That's even better!

We have a better covenant.

We have better blood.

Hebrews 9:14 says, "How much more will the blood of Christ, who through the eternal Spirit, offered Himself without blemish to God, cleanse your conscience from dead works to serve the living God?"

Not only does the blood of Jesus cleanse us, but it EMPOWERS us to SERVE the living God. We can't be cleansed without His blood; and we don't have the capacity or strength to serve Him, except through His blood. His blood, which releases His grace, cleanses AND empowers us for this walk with Him that we all so desire!

YOU HAVE IT SO MUCH BETTER!

Jesus says to you and me in Luke 10:19, "Behold, I give you authority to trample on serpents and scorpions and over all the power of the enemy, and NOTHING SHALL BY ANY MEANS HURT YOU."

I like the word, nothing there. It is similar to Isaiah 54:17, where he says, "NO weapon formed against you shall prosper." It is all-inclusive and definite! It covers every aspect of our lives: whether it be weapons of fear, weapons of terror, weapons of sickness and disease, weapons of debt, weapons of emotional pressure or weapons of financial pressure and stress—NO WEAPON CAN PROSPER!

Now let me show you how this promise becomes real in our lives.

1. First, we must understand the powerful Passover of the Old Covenant.

In Exodus 12, the children of Israel are commanded by God to kill a lamb and put the blood over the doorposts of their houses so that when the plague of death came to strike down the first born of each house, it would PASS OVER them. "And when I see the blood, I will pass over you; and the plague shall not be on you to destroy you" (Exodus 12:13).

God honored the blood of a lamb. He brought divine protection to the children of Israel through the blood of the PASSOVER lamb. This is understood as *a blood covenant.*

2. Next we need to understand God's New Covenant Passover Lamb.

In 1 Corinthians 5:7, Jesus Christ is called our Passover lamb. So He is to us what the Passover lamb of Exodus was to the children of Israel: providing divine protection and deliverance from plagues, destruction, and bondage. I AM IN AWE THAT HE WOULD BECOME OUR LAMB.

3. Next we need to understand the difference between these Passover lambs, and these covenants. The NEW covenant is BETTER than the old.

In Hebrews 8:6, it says that Jesus has obtained a "more excellent ministry, and He is the Mediator of a BETTER COVENANT, which was established on BETTER PROMISES."

Notice, the differences here between the Old Covenant, which was very powerful, versus the New Covenant:

a. The New Covenant is MORE EXCELLENT.

b. It is a BETTER COVENANT.

c. It has BETTER PROMISES.

When I go to the store and see a product like laundry detergent that says it is "NEW and IMPROVED," it means that it has to do AT LEAST what the old product did AND THEN SOME. When we accept that we have the Blood of Jesus as our PASSOVER, we must understand that the New Covenant will do AT LEAST as much as the old one did, AND THEN SOME.

This is a BETTER covenant, with BETTER promises. Therefore, you and I can expect BETTER results! Why? Because it was established by better blood—the blood of the perfect Lamb, the Son of God. (Hebrews 9:11–13)

Notice what the OLD COVENANT could do and expect MORE!

Under the OLD COVENANT, the children of Israel enjoyed **supernatural protection** from the enemies of death and terror (Exodus 12:13). They enjoyed **supernatural deliverance** from the most ferocious army in the world, the Egyptians (Exodus 15:13). The children of Israel enjoyed **supernatural provision**, by the plundering of the Egyptian's wealth, which was transferred into the hands of Israel (Exodus 12:35). And they enjoyed **supernatural health**, as they left Egypt. "There was not **a sick**, or **feeble person among them**" (Ps 105:37).

In the midst of any and all circumstances occurring in our world or your life, you can enjoy God's divine promises just like the children of Israel did, because of the grace that flows from this new blood covenant!

Chapter Five

Experience This More Than Amazing Grace

Now, how do we experience the benefits of this BETTER COVENANT with BETTER PROMISES?

1. We must know that this covenant went into effect the day Jesus died on the cross. "For a covenant is in force after men are dead, since it has no power at all while the one who made it lives" (Hebrews 9:17).

2. Come boldly to the throne of God's grace and make your request known to Him (Hebrews 4:15–16). The throne of grace is open wide! There is no shortage of mercy; no shortage of grace; no shortage of help in our time of need. Go to Him now. Go to Him tonight. Go to Him in your darkest moment; or go to Him to simply ask for His help with your present situation. His fountain of grace never runs dry.

How do we go to this throne of grace?

"Therefore, brethren, having boldness to enter the Holiest by the blood of Jesus" (Hebrews 10:19). We don't come to Him by begging and crying, or because we feel we've prayed long enough or been holy enough. We enter the holiest *place*; but we don't enter by being the holiest *people*! We enter by the blood of Jesus! His blood makes us righteous—giving us the right to stand before His throne without guilt, inferiority, shame, or fear.

3. Declare it with our mouths. Romans 10:10 says, "with the mouth confession is made unto salvation," salvation meaning deliverance, wholeness, and protection. Declare today that the blood of Jesus protects you, delivers you, heals you, and prospers you!

4. Remember this covenant by celebrating communion— reinforcing before ourselves, before God, and before all the devils in this world that we are under grace—God's divine promises and enablement—through the blood of Jesus. There is a unique and magnificent power released every time you receive the body and blood of Jesus in communion. You don't have to wait for a special service. You can receive this right in your home.

5. Believe the last three words Jesus said on the cross: IT IS FINISHED! When He died on the cross, He established this new covenant. Jesus did it all. All that is left for us to do is rest in His finished work. When you do, you will see His MORE THAN amazing promises manifest in your life!

Chapter Six

Don't Fall Short
of the Grace

*"See to it that no one falls short of the grace of God;
that no root of bitterness springing up causes trouble,
and by it many be defiled" (Hebrews 12:15).*

What does it mean to fall short of the grace of God? We
have overcomplicated this simple truth.

To *fall short* actually means: "to be inferior to," "to live
beneath," or "to be smaller than." What this verse is saying
to me here is: Don't face anything in life without applying
grace to it! Nothing in life was meant to be faced without
God's grace. When you try life without grace, you'll come
up on the short end of things, and you'll get bitter.

Another way to look at it is: Don't live beneath what Jesus
paid for you to have. Don't live smaller than the big life
that grace will create for you!

Grace makes you go big! Grace brings you into the promises of God without a struggle. Grace brings you into a life
beyond your wildest dreams!

God has a life much bigger and greater than you've ever imagined; both in this life and in the life to come. We don't get there by what we do; but by what He did for us.

What is *amazing* is that we all know, deep down, that we were created for something bigger than ourselves. We know this because, as Solomon writes, God **"has set eternity in our heart"** (Ecclesiastes 3:11).

Many people today are living with inner dissatisfaction, without faith in God at all. But it's not because they are completely immoral or ungodly. It's because they have not found or heard about a God big enough to make sense of the things in life, big enough to allow them to make mistakes without damnation or punishment, big enough to awaken their highest destiny, and big enough to not need to threaten or scare them into accepting Him.

To believe in a smaller God than who He really is, is to fall short of the grace of God.

If we believe we are one mistake away from His wrath or judgement, this is falling short of His grace. Because it's less than what grace has done for us.

We don't fall short and live a small life because of something we DO. We live a small life, falling short of His grace, because of something we BELIEVE.

When we believe life is a struggle to please Him, a struggle to receive His love and acceptance, a struggle to receive His favor and goodness, we are living inferior (falling short) of the grace of God.

When we believe that our mistakes are greater than His grace, we will live a smaller life than what He intends for us. This will make us bitter.

When we believe that what people have done TO us, is greater than what God has done FOR us, we will fall short of the life He intended. This too will make us bitter.

Bitterness is the evidence that we are not applying God's grace to our life or situation.

Notice how Joseph understood God's grace (that would be fully realized in Christ Jesus) AFTER his brothers had sold him into slavery.

"You intended to harm me, but God intended it for good to accomplish what is now being done, the saving of many lives" (Genesis 50:20 NIV).

He understood that God's plans were bigger than man's plots. No matter what man did TO him, Joseph knew God was doing something FOR him and through him. This understanding of God's grace and goodness prevented him from being bitter. As you apply these truths of grace, you will not fall short, live small, or be bitter ever again!

Chapter Seven

You Have Arrived

"By now it was dark, and He had not yet come to them" (John 6:17).

HAVE YOU EVER FELT THAT? IT'S DARK, and God hasn't seemed to show up in your life or situation yet? A little boy, afraid of the dark, was asked by his mother to go out to the back porch and bring her the broom.

The little boy turned to his mother and said, "Mama, I don't want to go out there. It's dark!" His mother smiled reassuringly at her son, "You don't have to be afraid of the dark. Jesus is out there. He'll look after you and protect you," she explained.

The little boy looked at his mother real hard and asked, "Are you sure He's out there?" "Yes, I'm sure. He is everywhere, and He is always ready to help you when you need Him," she said.

He thought about it for a minute, and then went to the back door and cracked it a little. Peering out into the darkness, without going too far, he yelled, "Jesus? If you're really out there, can you hand me the broom?"

Do you need Jesus to reach out to you today?

Back to the storm in John, chapter 6.

The disciples were struggling for hours and getting nowhere. This produced fear in their hearts. Often times, fear will come when we struggle and struggle, making no progress. God's grace delivers us from fear.

"And the sea arose by reason of a great storm that blew" (verse 18).

When they started out, it was calm. The storm on this sea could hit suddenly and unexpectedly. That's how life is, isn't it? Storms in life can seem to hit suddenly: trouble, a trial, sickness, financial difficulty, a marriage problem. Bam!

Verse 19 continues, "When they had rowed about three or four miles, they saw Jesus approaching the boat, walking on the water, and they were frightened."

THEY HAD BEEN STRUGGLING FOR six to nine—hours—from dark almost until dawn.

Referencing this storm, it says in Mark 6:48, "Jesus saw them straining at the oars before dawn." He saw that they were in serious trouble. He saw them being battered as they rowed. When He saw that His disciples were in trouble, Jesus said, "It is I. Do not be afraid." (Verse 20)

Two things delivered them from fear:

1. They Heard His Word. The Word of God delivered them from fear: "It is I."

They couldn't see because of the storm and the darkness. BUT they could hear!

2. They willingly received Him. (vs. 21) This is the grace of God.

And that's when the greatest miracle happened! **When He got in the boat, they were immediately at their destination.**

If you study the map of this journey, you will find that from one end of the sea to the other, it is about seven miles. When the storm hit, and they were exhausted at rowing, they had only gotten "three or four miles" or halfway across.

THEIR OWN POWER COULD ONLY GET THEM HALFWAY AND NO FURTHER.

The Law, our striving, and our struggling can't get us to the other side. ONLY GOD'S GRACE can. It took them six to nine hours to row halfway, and they were exhausted and stuck in the middle of the sea. They were halfway there, and they were about to drown! (Ever felt like that?)

But when they received Jesus into their boat, they were immediately there. Despite all their rowing, they were about to die! BUT when they received Him into the boat, they were immediately at their destination.

This is the miracle of God's grace.

I wrote at the beginning of this book: When I hear the echo of those words Jesus spoke hanging from the cross—"IT IS FINISHED," I realize I have arrived. No more striving. No more sweating.

This is grace.

"Then they willingly received Him into the boat, and immediately the boat was at the land where they were going" (John 6:21).

This is grace: no more striving to "get there"; no more sweating, pleading, begging, or straining at the oars!

> "Thou Framer of the light and dark,
> Steer through the tempest thine own ark;
> Amid the howling wintry sea,
> We are in port, if we have thee."
>
> —Henry Troth Coates

So the little boat was propelled by the invisible power of grace—gliding through the settled waters. While they were in awe of what had happened they found themselves pleasantly surprised, at their destination!

Are you ready to be pleasantly surprised by arriving at your destination? Pleasantly surprised at what God can do in your life? I know I am. I know you are, too!

How much longer do you want to struggle with your journey, in your own power? How much longer do you want to struggle with your finances, your marriage, or your health?

Jesus can be walking on the water around you. It's a great miracle to watch Him do amazing things around us, but He wants to do great things FOR US.

When you RECEIVE HIM WILLINGLY—take all of Him in His glorious grace FREELY—then your struggle ends.

No more fear.

No more struggle.

No more straining at the oars.

YOU ARE THERE.

Chapter Eight

The Promise

The way of grace and faith for all believers is vividly illustrated in the story of Abraham, Isaac, and Ishmael.

God made a promise. Abraham and Sarah could hardly take it, waiting and waiting.

"Then God said to Abraham, "As for Sarai your wife, you shall not call her name Sarai, but Sarah shall be her name. I will bless her, and indeed I will give you a son by her. Then I will bless her, and she shall be a mother of nations; kings of peoples will come from her" (Genesis 17:15–16).

How many years have now passed without God fulfilling His promise? Twenty-five years!

"Then Abraham fell on his face and laughed, and said in his heart, "Will a child be born to a man one hundred years old? And will Sarah, who is ninety years old, bear a child?" (vs. 17)

Abraham is at the end of himself. He laughs at the promise because it seemed like it could never happen.

For Sarah, the waiting for this preposterous promise created deep pain within. So she took matters into her own hands and said to Abraham, "The Lord has kept me from having children. Go, sleep with my slave; perhaps I can build a family through her" (Genesis 16:2 NIV).

And, Abraham agreed to what Sarah said. (She probably didn't have to try too hard to convince him! Uh oh!)

Later, verse 12 describes this son of their fleshly effort named Ishmael: "He will be a wild donkey of a man; his hand will be against everyone and everyone's hand against him, and he will live in hostility toward all his brothers."

When we strive to MAKE God's promises come to pass, we will make wild donkeys (asses!) of ourselves.

Abraham, in his own effort to bring God's promise to pass, went along with Sarah's suggestion—thinking that God would now bring about His promise through Ishmael.

They had fallen into the trap that so many believers fall into as they start out on the journey of faith in God's promises.

They had misunderstood the meaning of a promise. They had interpreted God's promises as a challenge to them to struggle to get Him to do it.

That is NOT the Gospel and not the GRACE LIFE that God wants us to live. Think about it this way: The promise that a parent makes to a child of a new cell phone at Christmas, is not a challenge to the child to obtain a phone by December 25th. It is an ANNOUNCEMENT of what the parents plan to do without the child's help. Grace is an announcement of what God has done; not a challenge to us to somehow get Him to do it.

We are trying to help God. He doesn't need our help. He simply needs us to take Him at His Word, and rest confidently in the fact that HE IS WATCHING OVER HIS WORD TO PERFORM IT! (Jeremiah 1:12)

For many, the Christian life has become a massive struggle to achieve God's will and manifest His promises, rather than peacefully resting in His character of faithfulness.

Although they would probably not admit it, there are countless Christians who are disillusioned with modern Christianity. They were promised a joy-filled, blessed life, and peace in the midst of trouble. And it simply hasn't materialized. It's demoralizing. And that's how the enemy likes it.

Many people subtly simmer with a quiet anger at God, feeling that He has tricked them—that He advertised His kingdom of promises and joy in Scripture, but failed to follow through in doing what He said.

But we don't have to live in this quiet anger. We can live in true joy. WE ARE CALLED TO ENTER INTO HIS REST. This is the rest of faith.

This life of grace is not about the promises we make to God; but rather the promises He makes to us!

When Isaac, the son of God's promise, is finally born, Sarah says, "God has made laughter for me; everyone who hears will laugh with me" (Genesis 21:6). One of the differences between grace and legalism is that grace produces the laughter of true joy and awe, while legalism produces the sarcastic laugh of disappointment and skepticism.

We are sons of Isaac—BORN TO LAUGH and REJOICE—with true joy, according to Galatians 4:29.

BUT we've been acting more like sons of Ishmael, struggling to live for God—struggling to be happy, struggling to pray, to live holy and to earn God's affection. We have felt like we were on the outside, looking in, having to perform or produce for God in order to find His acceptance. We negotiate and promise God we will serve Him, in exchange for blessings or answered prayer. That's not the way of grace. We don't have to make a deal with God. He has made the deal with us, through the blood of Jesus. All we have to do is receive!

Chapter Nine

The Real Fight

THE REAL FIGHT NOW IS to reject the religion of Ishmael, the religion of striving and sorrow; and accept the faith of Isaac, the religion of rest, laughter and trust.

In Genesis 3:16, Adam and Eve were cursed with a life of struggle: "IN SORROW YOU SHALL CONCEIVE." Contrast that with the life of Jesus—who had more joy than anyone (Hebrews 1:9).

And as He is, so are we, in this life! (1 John 4:17)

You have a new DNA. You're not of Eve anymore, giving birth in sorrow and living in sorrow. You're of Sarah, giving birth in laughter. God does it. It comes naturally.

Trust that *God* will bring His promises to pass in your life. *He* will do it. Simply rest in faith—faith in His amazing grace.

The Christian life is NOT living FOR God, but living FROM God.

"I have been crucified with Christ; and it is no longer I who live, but Christ lives in me; and the life which I now live in the flesh I live by faith in the Son of God, who loved me and gave Himself up for me" (Galatians 2:20).

When I first got saved, I didn't stress out, pray for hours, or fast for 40 days to be saved. I simply accepted the arms of Jesus that he put around me. I simply accepted His embrace—*while* I was a child of the devil. Now that I'm a child of God, why do I struggle now, stress so much, sweat so much, worry so much, or wonder, "Is God going to do it? Is God going to answer?" If He gave me the greatest gift of salvation freely, why would He hold back any of His gifts? This truth will take the pressure off of you.

You didn't get saved in your own power and in your own strength, and you're not going to fulfill God's purpose in your own power and in your own strength. And you don't have to.

Relax. Your struggle is over.

LIKE MIKE

Back in the Michael Jordan era of basketball, everybody wanted to "be like Mike." Maybe you remember the song "If I could be like Mike." Yet, no matter how good of a basketball player you could be, you just can't be like Mike! Even if you were to wear MJ's shoes, drink MJ's Gatorade, and wear MJ's Hanes underwear, there's still no way to "be like Mike."

But what if it were possible to unzip your body and have Michael Jordan—in his prime—come live inside of you?

What if on the outside you're you, but on the inside of you lives Michael Jordan? Then you could jump like Mike, soar like Mike, and score like Mike! Right?

That's fun to imagine, yet we know it's impossible for him to live inside of us.

Without him living inside of you, you can try and try but you'll never jump like him, score like him, or make money like him.

Do you see where I'm going with this?

So many Christians try and try but fail at living like Christ or loving like Christ. So many are struggling in life to be like Jesus, but failing. You can have a Bible, but you won't be like Jesus. You can lift your hands, but you won't be like Jesus. You can fast until you're so skinny you have to run around in the shower just to get wet—yet still, you find, you're not like Jesus.

Christians strive and struggle in their own strength to be Christlike, only to stumble and fall short time and time again.

However, it IS possible for GOD to live inside of you, and it will take just that for you to be like Him.

Chapter Ten

The Spirit

Many Christians try to obey God and live holy out of sheer willpower, and they fail, burn out, and quit. You'll never give up when you realize, it's God who began this good work in you; He will finish it (Philippians 1:6).

We cannot fulfill God's purpose for our lives without the power and presence of the Holy Spirit.

When I think of a man who fulfilled God's purpose for his life, I think of the Apostle Peter, after he understood the spirit of grace. We can all relate to Peter.

While he's following Jesus, we see Peter make mistake after mistake, blunder after blunder. But God never gives up on him! That's grace. What's even MORE than amazing grace, is that He comes to live inside of Peter (and us). That's when things get exciting! That's when things change. That's when Peter begins to walk in His destiny!

But before we look at the turnaround in his life, let's look at five things that caused Peter to miss out, for a while, on God's purpose for his life. And then how God turned it around!

1. Peter has his own agenda. In Matthew 16, Jesus tells His disciples that He must go to Jerusalem, suffer many things, be killed, and He would rise on the third day (verse 21). But Peter rebukes Him, saying, "Far be it from you Lord. This shall not happen to you" (verse 22). Peter is basically saying, "No, Lord, that's not my plan, not my agenda."

Notice what Jesus says: "Get behind me, Satan. You are an offense to me, because you are not mindful of the things of God, but of the things of men." This is blunder number one.

2. Peter made promises to God he couldn't keep. Have you ever done that? "I promise God, I'm going to pray every day, treat that person better, stop getting mad, and be a better husband or wife."

In Luke 22, Jesus said to Peter, "Before the cock crows, you're going to deny me three times." Peter responded, "No, even though everyone else denies you, I'm never going to deny you" (Verse 34).

Peter was living his life based on the promises he made to God, rather than based on the promises God made to him. Live your life that way, and you'll burn out. But if you live based on the promises God makes to us, you're going to experience the purpose, power and blessing of God every day of your life.

3. Peter allowed his emotions to get the best of him. When confronted with the soldiers that came to take Jesus away, Peter pulls out his sword and cuts the servant's ear off (John 18:10). Peter whips out his sword when he's mad and starts cutting people down to size. Know anyone like that? Haha!

4. Peter falls into the comparison trap (John 21:19–20). Jesus tells Peter to follow him. Then Peter replies to Jesus, (about John), "But Lord, what about this man?" Jesus basically responds by saying: Stop comparing yourself to anyone else; focus on what I've called you to do.

5. Peter runs when the pressure comes. When Jesus goes to the cross, Peter runs away. One historian described it saying, "He ran so fast out of the presence of Jesus' crucifixion, we didn't think he'd ever come back!"

Can you locate yourself in one or more of the areas that Peter struggled with? I know I can. But there is hope, because of God's more than amazing grace!

Here's a man who has his own agenda, makes promises he can't keep, compares himself to others, lets his emotions get the best of him, and runs from persecution and opposition! But even when he denies the Lord three times, and turns AWAY from Jesus, Jesus turns TOWARD Peter with acceptance and love (Luke 22:61). This is grace!

THEN...

In Acts, chapter two, with the sound of a rushing wind, Peter along with the others gathered, was filled with the Holy Spirit—and God's grace begins to work on the inside of him!

What happens to Peter after he's filled with the Holy Spirit?

1. The Bible made sense to him. Peter, who could not put two sentences together without putting his foot in his mouth before, stands up and speaks brilliantly to the thousands that were gathered (verse 14).

For the next 30 verses, he quotes the book of Joel. Peter hasn't quoted a Bible verse in three years! But after he's filled with the Holy Spirit, he's quoting verse after verse and applying it to life.

2. He was empowered to do what he wasn't able to do before in his own power. Peter could stand up and take his rightful place in the kingdom of God. He was able to speak on behalf of Jesus; (he had only spoken on his own behalf up to this point).

3. He steps into his destiny. Three Thousand people were saved that day through Peter's preaching. Prior to this, he always spoke just to save himself. Now he is helping to save others by the same grace that saved him!

4. He introduced the world to a promise-based Christianity. Peter says, "This *promise* is for you and your children and as many as the Lord has called to himself" (Acts 2:39).

He saw that life was no longer about the promises that he made to God. Now his life was about the promises that God made to him!

As you embrace the life of grace and awaken to the spirit of grace living in you and through you, you will stop struggling to get by. You'll stop making failed promises to God and start living in God's promises to you. You'll start living FROM God, rather than just FOR God. You'll find yourself ARRIVING at the destination of God's MORE THAN AMAZING GRACE in your life!

No more striving. No more sweating. No more trying to get right with God through your efforts. No more making promises to be holy, to be better, to clean up your act; no more trying to pick up the pieces of a broken life. He makes you holy. He makes you better. He cleans you up. He picks up the broken pieces and makes you whole again. IT IS FINISHED. By God's grace, you have arrived!

Are you ready to live a life beyond your wildest dreams? It all begins as we discover and trust in this MORE THAN AMAZING GRACE!

Chapter Eleven

The State of Grace

The Gospel of grace is an invitation to happiness. We're not inviting people to a funeral, but to a wedding feast!

So why is the world so unhappy?

Children singing, "Jesus loves me, this I know" has been replaced with, "Hey mom, my medication is wearing off."

One recent study showed that preschoolers shockingly lead the growth in antidepressant use. It showed their usage up more than 50 percent among children five and under over the last several years. (I am not saying that medication is wrong. I just want to bring awareness to this epidemic and believe with people for freedom and healing.) The use of paroxetine and other antidepressant medications continues to grow by about 10 percent annually among children and adolescents, according to a study published in an issue of *Psychiatric Services*.

In a four-year span in recent years, the fastest-growing segment of users were found to be preschoolers aged 0–5 years, with use among girls doubling and use among boys growing by over 60 percent.

At the time of this writing, 80 percent of the world's painkillers are consumed in America. A death by overdose occurs every 19 minutes on average.

But what has made this world, even among believers, so sad? Where are kids learning to be so discouraged and depressed? In the home. People are unhappy at home.

So I'm announcing that it's TIME TO MOVE; not from your house, but from your state. Not from one of the 50 states in America—**but it's time to move to THE STATE OF GRACE.** We are all relocating today. We are moving to the state of grace! Ready? God's grace brings joy. It will make you happy. That's why we all need to discover the grace that not only saves, but brings joy! Men, women, dads, moms, boys and girls, grandmas and grandpas, it's time to live in the state of grace.

You see, the greatest enemy of the church is not necessarily the devil. It's misunderstanding grace. It's legalism and self-righteousness.

No wonder there are so many non-believers who don't want anything to do with church. It's not that they hate God. They hate hypocrisy, legalism, religion.

Churches are often filled with people that are unhappy and even bitter. A joyless church (just like a joyless Christian) is one that has not discovered the grace of God.

So where is this state of grace located? What is the address? Well, its address is Ephesians 2:6. "We are seated with

Christ in heavenly places!" We are positioned with Jesus, at the throne of grace. (Hebrews 4:16)

It's the place where God rules over all principalities and powers and reigns in this life. Romans 5:17 says that it's "through the abundance of grace and the gift of righteousness that WE reign as kings in THIS LIFE."

If this is where we are seated NOW, why aren't we experiencing it? Why are so many Christians living up and down; filled with anxiety or despair? Why are so many discouraged and feeling defeated by life's trials?

We've been living in the wrong state! And it's time to move! We've been living in the State of Despair; the State of Confusion; the State of Fear. And it's ending today! We're moving to the State of Grace!

To be seated with Christ, means we are in the place of absolute and complete victory.

After Jesus died and rose from the dead, He sat down at the right hand of the Father in heaven. All that He needed to do for our salvation and victory was FINISHED. And now, we are seated with Him and in Him.

Notice, we don't have to fight or beg, borrow or steal our way into this seat. We don't have to kick someone out to get into this seat. We're not TRYING to be seated. We

ARE seated. If you are in Christ (by simply being born-again), you are in the seat of victory, because that's where He is!

So we are not living to try to get the victory. We are living FROM the victory. The battle is simply to BELIEVE. Our battle is to hold fast to what Jesus has already done for us and given to us. This is the state of grace!

When you understand this, it will change how you pray. We will stop begging, whining, or asking God for the victory; and instead praise Him that we got it! Say it: "I already got it!" Instead of asking God for victory, renew your mind to what He already said you are and you have, and that will conform you to His image—while we look into the mirror of God's Word—believing what He already said we are, in Him, we are conformed to that image (2 Corinthians 3:18). Instead of getting depressed about the trial you're in or the lack you're facing, awaken to the fact that you have the victory and its only a matter of time before you SEE it. Believe you HAVE received it and you will soon see it (Mark 11:24).

We don't have to beg and struggle and cry to get God to do what He said. We must believe: It's already done in Him. And we're in Him!

Are you ready to give up the life of struggle—of ups and downs, hardly ever feeling like you're happy or pleasing to

God? I know you are. Dare to believe that you are seated with Christ! And make this your declaration from this moment forward:

"I declare today that I am moving from the state of fear, unhappiness, condemnation, and despair! My address has changed. The enemy won't find me there anymore. I have moved from Unhappiness Avenue; Condemnation Court, and Loser Lane! I have moved to the State of Grace. That's where I live now. I am seated with Christ in Heavenly places. I no longer answer to the names the enemy tried to label me with. I am a victor not a victim. I answer to the name of Victor or Victoria! More than a Conqueror! World Dominator! Reigning in Life, in Jesus' Name!"

Now get ready. Expect to experience God's more than amazing grace, both today and forever! Amen.

Receive the Gift of Salvation

Perhaps you have never received Jesus Christ as your Savior and Lord, or you're not sure you will go to heaven when you die. Well, you can be sure today.

Or perhaps you have tried to be good, and you thought, "If I am good enough, if I go to church or try to clean up my life, then I will be saved." But none of that will save you. There is only one way to get to heaven—by accepting forgiveness and the gift of salvation, through the sacrifice Jesus made on the Cross.

I want to lead you in this prayer of faith, and something miraculous is going to happen in your heart.

Pray this out loud:

"Heavenly Father, I accept Jesus Christ into my life as my Savior and Lord. I believe Jesus died for my sins and rose from the dead. I receive the forgiveness of my sins through the blood of Jesus. Take out my old heart, Lord, and give me a new heart and a new life. Make me born again. By grace I am saved today through faith. I freely accept your love and grace to enable me to walk with you all the days of my life, in Jesus' Name. Amen!"

Now listen. That is just the beginning.

God wants you to grow. He wants you to move forward and live in His purpose for your life. When we get born again, we start a brand-new life. You don't have to live like you used to live. But we all need help to live out this new life in Christ. If you have just received Jesus as your Savior and Lord, contact our prayer center at 847-645-9700 and let us know. I want to help you.

Next Steps

Read the Bible and talk to God. God has a great plan for your life. He loves you and wants the best for you. You are His child now. You are in the family of God today. Your life will never be the same again!

Now thank Him for making you His child. And don't doubt! You are a child of God right now! John 1:12 says, "To as many as received Jesus, to them He gave the right to become sons and daughters of God."

Next, you should find a good Bible-believing church, where you can grow together with other believers and find your place in a spiritual home! It is my pleasure to welcome you into the family of God!

The Baptism in the Holy Spirit

The baptism in the Holy Spirit is an empowerment for service that takes place in the life of the Christian (Acts 1:5,8). In it, we are immersed in the Spirit's life and power. To illustrate, if we drank water from a glass, then the water would be inside of us. However, if we went to the beach and stepped into the ocean, then we would be in the water. We receive, as it were, a drink of the Holy Spirit when we are saved, but when we are baptized in the Spirit, it is as if that initial drink becomes an ocean that completely surrounds us. Just as the indwelling Spirit that Christians receive when they are saved reproduces the life of Jesus, so the outpoured, or baptizing Spirit reproduces the ministry of Jesus, including miracles and healings.

Why Do We Need the Baptism in the Holy Spirit? We need a power beyond ourselves for service and ministry in Christ's Kingdom. When Jesus gave the Great Commission (Matthew 28:19–20), He knew that His disciples could not fulfill it in their own power. Therefore, He had a special gift in store for them: It was His plan to give them the same power that He had—the power of the Spirit of God.

So, immediately after giving them the Great Commission, Jesus commanded His disciples not to leave Jerusalem, but to wait for what the Father promised, "which," He said, "you heard of from Me; for John baptized with water, but you shall be baptized with the Holy Spirit not many days from now" (Acts 1:4–5). He further promised, "You shall receive power when the Holy Spirit has come upon you; and you shall be My witnesses both in Jerusalem, and in all Judea and Samaria, and even to the remotest part of the earth" (Acts 1:8).

The disciples gathered, and "suddenly there came from heaven a noise like a violent, rushing wind, and it filled the whole house where they were sitting. And there appeared to them tongues as of fire distributing themselves, and they rested on each one of them. And they were filled with the Holy Spirit and began to speak with other tongues, as the Spirit was giving them utterance" (Acts 2:3,4).

Then Peter explained to the crowd that gathered that they were seeing the working of God's Spirit and told them about Jesus. This is the same gift that God wants for you!

How Do I Receive the Baptism in the Holy Spirit? First, once you have accepted Jesus Christ as your Savior you simply ask God to baptize you in the Holy Spirit. The Bible says, "Ask, and it shall be given to you" (Luke 11:9). Second, believe you have in fact received this gift from God. The Apostle Paul, said, "Did you receive the Spirit by the works of the law, or by hearing with faith?" (Galatians 3:2). The answer, obviously, is faith. You have to believe that if you ask, you will receive. Pray this prayer if you desire to receive the baptism in God's Holy Spirit:

"Heavenly Father, at this moment I come to You. I thank You that Jesus saved me. Baptize me now in the Holy Spirit. I receive the baptism in the Holy Spirit right now by faith in Your Word. And right now I receive the gift of speaking in other tongues. May I be empowered to serve you in a new dimension from this day forward. Thank You, Father, for baptizing me in Your Holy Spirit. Amen."

Now, having asked and received, begin to practice the power of the Spirit. An ideal place to begin is where the first apostles did, praising God in your brand-new tongue. To do this, begin praising God out loud in whatever words God brings to you by the Spirit's inspiration. Tell Him how much you love Him. Thank Him, worship Him, and yield your voice to Him. Now let Him give you new words of praise you never heard before. Praise Him with those words, too. You'll find that this can be a very rewarding experience of communication with God that will build up your faith. Continue to pray to God each day in the language that the Holy Spirit has given you.

If you have more questions about the Holy Spirit and His gifts, contact our Prayer Center at 847-645-9700, so we can pray with you according to God's Word.